D1163590

The Hampton Album

44 photographs by Frances B. Johnston from an album of Hampton Institute

with an introduction and a note on the photographer by Lincoln Kirstein

The Museum of Modern Art, New York

Distributed by Doubleday & Co., Inc. Garden City, New York

11 WEST 53 STREET, NEW YORK, N.Y. 10019

LIBRARY OF CONGRESS CATALOGUE CARD NUMBER 65-29016

PRINTED IN THE UNITED STATES OF AMERICA.

ACKNOWLEDGMENTS

The museum gratefully acknowledges its indebtedness to Lincoln Kirstein, who through the good offices of Monroe Wheeler brought The Hampton Album to the attention of the Department of Photography, and who subsequently made the generous gift of this unique and challenging work to the Museum's Collection. In addition Mr. Kirstein's advice was of inestimable help in editing, from the 159 plates in the original album, the 44 which are reproduced here.

The original platinum prints which are reproduced here were exhibited in the Museum's Edward Steichen Photography Center in January 1966.

The historical reality so poignantly described in Frances Johnston's pictures is of course in fundamental contrast to the reality of Hampton Institute today. In the sixty-five years since these pictures were made, Hampton has advanced from a primarily vocational school to a fully accredited liberal arts college with an international faculty and student body, and a curriculum responsive to the intellectual and social commitments of our own day.

John Szarkowski,
Director, Department of Photography

Titles are those on the original tissue over-lays for each photograph in the Album.

COVER: *"Stairway of Treasurer's Residence. Students at work."*
PAGE 1: *"Southern Water-front"*
PAGE 2: *"About 400 Students in Memorial Chapel"*

FOREWORD

THESE PHOTOGRAPHS, originally made for the Paris Exposition of 1900 by Frances Benjamin Johnston as part of an exhibition demonstrating contemporary life of the American Negro, comprise a body of work almost inexhaustibly revealing. In the following brief initial sketch of but one facet of Miss Johnston's vast labor, emphasis will be on her visual capacity rather than, as might be more fitting, her talent as a journalist, as portraitist, as architectural historian, or as a fascinating figure of American feminism in the decades from 1882 to 1952. The immediate subject of this particular photographic essay is a famous educational institution, thirty-one years old when these pictures were taken. Its subsequent history has more than amply fulfilled all promises Miss Johnston captured in 1899 and 1900. Present events, together with its approaching centennial celebration, conspire to place Hampton Institute today in a uniquely symbolic position in American social history and educational philosophy. It would take a study in depth by an able, generously endowed historian to do justice to the place of the Institute in the era of Reconstruction in its first steps after the Civil War towards the essential, not the legal, enfranchisement of the Negro. Its extraordinarily successful experiment in the training of black and American Indian youth, the triumph of an integrated coeducational system of learning-by-doing in the domestic and agricultural arts and crafts, enabling them to teach others to do likewise, demands its own massive volume. It is more than likely that social and historical factors outweigh purely aesthetic values in Miss Johnston's plates, but here, upon the limited wall-space of a museum and within the few pages of this brochure, let us, primarily, discover these pictures. They are amazingly evocative. With a sketchy background they can tell us what more detailed facts, dates and statistics can only reinforce or corroborate. Miss Johnston's extraordinary talent as a photographer, early recognized in her own lifetime, if all but forgotten in ours, is apparent from a dozen of her picture stories and monographs which manifest her strength in formal or technical considerations, her delicacy and precision handling, her silvery light, and in her articulate, humane recognition of the condition of personality as in these portraits of persons and places in which she has synthesized and proclaimed the devotion, humility, sweetness and achievement of Hampton Institute.

During World War II, while stationed nearby, I found it pleasant to browse in old Washington bookstores. A plump, anonymous, leatherbound album, old and scuffed, came to hand in Lowdermilk's bookshop. How it had suffered its present decline, since it obviously had been put together with love and care, remained a mystery, together with the cause of its inception, its intention and its authorship. For more than twenty years it rested on private shelves to be shown to a few photographers or historians, all of whom immediately relished its precious savor. Now, through the good offices of the Department of Photography of The Museum of Modern Art, in whose collections this album has been deposited, these pictures may be generally shared. Miss Grace Mayer, the Museum's Curator of

Photography, was quick to discover the history of the photographs in the album, the album's authorship, and many of the facts that explain its social or artistic importance. Miss Eleanor A. Gilman, formerly Secretary of Hampton Institute and still informal Archivist, was the source of invaluable personal recollection. Mr. Paul Vanderbilt, now Curator, Iconographic Collections, State Historical Society of Wisconsin, knew Miss Johnston when he was Consultant in Iconography at the Library of Congress, and is the author of an appreciation of her work as an architectural historian. The Manuscript Division of the Library of Congress has over fifty boxes of unsorted Johnston materials awaiting the proper biographer. Dr. Alan Fern, Miss Virginia Daiker and Mr. Hirst D. Milhollen of the Division of Prints and Photographs of the Library supplied valuable data and personal memories of Miss Johnston.

HAMPTON INSTITUTE

The thing to be done was clear: to train selected Negro youth who should go out and teach and lead their people, first by example, by getting land and homes; to give them not a dollar that they could earn for themselves; to teach respect for labor, to replace stupid drudgery with skilled hands; and, to build up an industrial system, for the sake not only of self-support and industrial labor but also for the sake of character. And it seemed equally clear that the people of the country would support a wise work for the freedmen.

Thus wrote Samuel Chapman Armstrong, founder of Hampton Institute, originally known as the Hampton Normal and Agricultural Institute, born in 1839 on the island of Maui, Hawaii. From 1831 his New England missionary parents had labored in the Sandwich Islands, as the Hawaiian Islands were then known. Beginning in 1847, his father was Minister of Public Instruction, charged with the construction, maintenance and curriculum of some 500 native schools. Armstrong later wrote that "the emancipation, enfranchisement, and Christian civilization of a dark-skinned Polynesian people in many respects like the Negro race," adumbrated, and to a certain degree developed in detail, his eventual plan for Hampton, which was expressed in the keynote phrase "Education for Life" long before it was a fixed idea in his own mind. Young Armstrong came to the United States in 1860 to study at Williams College under the pioneer educator, Dr. Mark Hopkins. With the onrush of civil strife, Armstrong volunteered, spending the next two and one half years commanding Negro freedmen, and terminating his service as Colonel of the 8th and 9th U.S. Colored Troops. His men convinced him ". . . of the excellent qualities and capacities of the freedmen. . . . Their quick response to good treatment and to discipline was a constant surprise. Their tidiness, devotion to their duty and their leaders, their dash and daring in battle, and their ambition to improve—often studying their spelling books under fire—showed that slavery was a false though, for the time being, doubtless an educative condition, and that they deserved as good a chance as any people."

In three mystical, prophetic visions during the course of the war, Armstrong later wrote, the whole future design of a Negro school was revealed to him. He based the practical pattern on his experience of the Hilo Boarding and Manual Labor School (missionary) for boys, and the Lahaina-luna Seminary, an official Hawaiian Government academy which taught more advanced subjects. These schools instructed in but a single language, English, turning out good teachers able to build their own homes and to teach others to build theirs.

With the end of the war, Armstrong found himself in March 1866 at an historic site: Hampton, Virginia. Nearby was the former domain of Powhatan; a few miles away (Armstrong noted) the first American Indian child was baptized in the Christian faith. Also in this vicinity, the first sold Africans had been landed, and here also, General Butler's famous "contraband" order first liberated the slaves after Lincoln's Emancipation Proclamation. Armstrong was virtually Military Governor of ten of Virginia's Atlantic counties, with orders to command a large Negro demobilization cantonment, "to manage Negro affairs and adjust if possible the relations of the races." Thousands of Negro soldiers, returning from the Union Army, had no place to go. Many filtered back to their old plantations; many more did not wish to resume the conditions, if not the legality, of their former slavery. Through a committee of Boston ladies, some thousands found work in the North as domestic help. Armstrong was a friend of the Quaker laureate, John Greenleaf Whittier, and through other eminent religious, missionary and educational connections, was able to enlist an enlightened and liberal board of trustees for his proposed school. His own great personal energies and experience propelled his project at extraordinary speed. Hampton Institute opened in a left-over barracks in April 1868, with two white teachers and fifteen pupils. The girls lived in the wood building; the boys in tents. In 1870 it was incorporated by a special act of the State of Virginia, and began to enjoy some State, and later Federal funds, to be administered by the American Missionary Association. By 1899–1900, when Miss Johnston's pictures were made, there were already nearly a thousand students, of whom 135 were American Indians. In 1878, seventeen young Indians, former prisoners of war, had been brought from St. Petersburg, Florida, where they had been kept for three years. By the turn of the century there were nearly a hundred teachers and administrators. Among the group photographs in the album, there is a score of grandchildren of earlier graduates. A teacher, trained at Hampton, was reported by the *New-York Daily Tribune* (April 30, 1900) as being "happier over making his people grow onions than if he were running a pretentious sham of a university. As he expressed it; 'They could not talk much about astronomy, but they knew how to plough up geology.' "

Early proposals for Hampton were warmly supported by General (later President) James A. Garfield, Dr. Mark Hopkins, and many of the political and educational figures who were former Abolitionists. Whittier and the Society of Friends lent their support, and an Elementary School was named in honor of the poet. In return, the Hampton Battalion, although uniformed in regulation United States Army dress, drilled only with slim wooden batons, and no firearms.

Throughout the history of these early years, one comes upon many incidents of touching and charming behavior, poetically incarnating in the Institute's activities problems, conflicts, tensions crossing public events with private life, which inscribed the meaning of citizenship in the work and play of the students.

One of the most eminent of Hampton's graduates, Booker T. Washington, himself the founder of Tuskegee Institute, soon to become a sister institution, describes in his most eloquent autobiography, *Up From Slavery,* how, although he had his own pressing work in hand, General Armstrong persuaded his former pupil to return to Hampton, to assume charge of The Wigwam, a brick dormitory for Indian boys. He was the only person in the building not a redskin. The average Indian felt himself far superior to the whites, and immeasurably above the Negroes, since they had, themselves, never submitted to slavery, but also had owned large numbers of slaves. Off the reservations, they hated to have their long hair cut, to abandon wearing blankets and smoking pipe tobacco. Washington succeeded as house-master, modestly if ruefully adding as postscript: ". . . no white American ever thinks that any other race is wholly civilized until he wears the white man's clothes, eats the white man's food, speaks the white man's language, and professes the white man's religion."

From early days, one of the best-known extracurricular activities was the preservation of and a capella performance of Negro spirituals. From 1873 the Hampton Student Singers, and later the Hampton Quartet, appeared all over the country, earning funds for additions to the campus at Hampton. While students fired their own bricks in their own kiln, the singers "sang up" new buildings. They sang for President Grant in The White House and in Steinway Hall in New York, precursors of the long line of Negro vocalists who have kept their root traditions alive. An early graduate later remembered: "I think only General Armstrong called for plantation melodies in those days. He only could lift them out of the bitterness of the old life and make them ring with the promise of the new. . . ."

"His was," wrote Booker Washington in an article on the exhibit sent to Paris to show Hampton's work to the world, "a pious and lovable nature which delighted to do the Master's work by reaching out the hand of assistance to the lowest and most needy of the Master's children."

THE PHOTOGRAPHS

THE ALBUM may have been bound up for presentation purposes or to interest patrons in the work of the Institute or as a record of the Paris exhibition; it is more complete than similar materials at Hampton. The prints from large glass plates are carefully printed, one to a page, for the most part, each with a thin protective sheet upon which is written a brief explanatory title. A few pictures at the start, showing life of Indians on the reservations before enjoying the fruits of civilization and education, are not by her, nor is the earlier portrait of General Armstrong. A number of pictures she took are not included in the book, but were used in some of several articles appearing after 1900, concerning Hampton or the Paris show.

Miss Johnston came to Hampton in early December 1899. The weather was seasonably cool and fine, skies lightly overcast. The all but shadowless landscape, with its etched, leafless trees, gave the photographer a silvery half-light, a fine-grained taffeta shimmer that she was quick to grasp and able to render with unique subtlety and finesse.

It will be apparent from the sequence of Hampton views that fairly early in her career Miss Johnston had a developed personal vision and characteristic style. A simple monumentality in miniature, a sober austere placement of figures is already visible in the series on public schools in Washington, D.C., taken just prior to Hampton. As overture, she unfolds a lyric panorama of the riverfront, taken from the water (endpapers). A procession of school buildings, masts of small boats, stacks with thin smoke plumes, the heavy but luminous skies, unfold dramatically. This broad topographical parade is revealed in static, majestic calm. The Institute is presented as institution, graced by nature, but a permanent part of it—here, to stay. Such hath God and man wrought. More linear, graphic and monotone than any impressionist painting, her riverviews nevertheless remind one of Seurat's vibrant landscapes with roofs and tall chimneys. All her forms are clearly delineated in their air, separated with a defining discreteness, giving full value to their descriptive silhouettes.

She is at her best with people. Having commenced with land, sky and architecture, she congregates Hampton's student body in the handsome Italian Romanesque chapel, for a collective portrait. Here is her human overture—these hundreds of somber, grave, aware faces, fixed obediently, even hypnotically, if quite patiently upon the lens of the little lady. Considering the fact that this group photograph was taken indoors on a December day, requiring an extended exposure, one marvels to find how few forms are blurred—in this, or indeed in any of the prints. The sea of faces, each of which in the unreduced original possesses its own cameo characterization, reads as if transfixed in suspended, breathless animation. In the front row there is the heartening neighborliness of Negro and Indian lip and cheekbone; several arrestingly blonde heads accent some farther ranks. How beautifully has she captured the architectural detail, the pristine crispness of new, well-laid brick (fired in their own kiln); how well she maintains the balance between exterior and interior light, the outdoors streaming through the pierced tracery of the central supraporte; the tactile plasticity of mouldings; the pearly reflection of the electroliers. Every student is caught in unstrained ease: dignity, not stiffness.

And how quaintly hopeful is the tiny regiment of infants, pledging allegiance to their flag, ". . . and to the republic for which it stands, one nation, indivisible, with liberty and justice for all." It was already thirty-five years after Appomattox.

In her series of before-and-after contrasts Miss Johnston illuminates the radical changes Hampton made in the condition of the American community of colored men. We have the red man on the reservation, and the red man in football uniform. We have the black farmer "Ignorant of Nature's Laws" and then, his younger brother, "who (at Hampton) has studied Nature." Her capacity for a grave if unsentimental compassion approaches pathos. There must have been plenty of rude and primitive log cabins nearby then (as, indeed, now); without any contrivance or editing she could have observed scenes of Southern domestic life which might well have illustrated *Uncle Tom's Cabin, or Life Among the Lowly*. But with what relish does she turn her page to show the triumphant advance of progress, this new dispensation of freedmen, in their decent, neat, immaculately hygienic homes, frozen as in habitat groups, almost, but not quite entirely—believable. The sobriety of a Quaker ethic pervades her scenes like the mordant scent of fresh garden herbs. There are precious few smiling faces among the prim pinafores and starched blouses; no hair ribbon is out of place; no boot unshined. Everyone is on best behavior for the lady picture-taker. "Watch the birdie!" Without overt irony, we have the helpless yet not hopeless discrepancy in concept of the white Victorian ideal as criterion towards which all darker tribes and nations must perforce aspire. In how many homes at the time, in the South, indeed anywhere in the country, could one seize upon the divine domestic felicity of "The Hampton Graduate At Home," with burnished faces, polished cutlery, silk shawl slung over the shiny piano, the hand-painted oil of the Rockies?

American painting of the Golden Age of the nineteenth century was distinguished by the frontier virtues of candor, a sense of place and the sense of a nostalgic loneliness. In William Sidney Mount's beautiful *Music Hath Charms*, he saw a respectably dressed slave standing beyond the barndoor wherein the young masters play their jolly tunes. Bemused, he is separated but unaccusing. In Thomas Eakins' wonderful watercolor of a solemn small Negro boy dancing shyly, there is the same genial gravity and assertion in the cool appreciation of the subservient condition. Miss Johnston, like these noble and greatly gifted artists, managed to capture the tragic essence of necessity for all her lyrical contrasts. It is more difficult for a photographer to seize upon isolated symbols than for any synthesizing painter who may adapt facts and forms to his will by superior selection and enhancement. She had the gift of salvaging from accident metaphorical appurtenances: the old well-sweep, sign of dubious hygiene, and the new well-head at the back of the new house, repeating almost object for object, new against old. A picket fence replaces post-and-rail. The portraits of the working inhabitants could not be more contrastingly optimistic. We can only imagine with what righteous satisfaction the visual proof of such absolute and obvious amelioration was made and shown. That this admissible evidence was special, isolated, atypical and token rather than any widespread norm, is reflected at least partly, if unconsciously, in her wan metallic light, the suspended quality of movement, the pinched detail.

Miss Johnston must have developed her own techniques for handling schoolchildren. Strong-minded, masterful in the conservation of time and energy, she undoubtedly had the cooperation of the instructors and the students themselves, but she surely knew how to organize her groups. Each interior and exterior is framed by figures looking at the essential focus of the given occupation. She combines portions of related activity in a single plate. The subject of the day's work is chalked on the blackboard, captioned with an illustrative sketch. Would that she had had a motion-picture camera, but even lacking it, we follow her elegiac, pastoral drama. The somber, immaculate children ache and burn to learn.

In her "Class in American History," we behold a live Indian in full tribal regalia, posed on a model-stand, glorious as a thunderbird, isolated and strange as if he were stuffed and cased behind glass in the old Smithsonian Institution, that "attic of America." An Indian boy, uniformed in the official Battalion blue-and-gold version of a U.S. Trooper's dress, regards his blood-brother with awe. Behind perches another masterpiece of taxidermy, an American eagle, as ferociously disinfected and harmless as the patient students themselves. On the wall behind is a print of a Remington painting: cavalry, on their rough-riding way to exterminate rebellious Piute or Ojibwa. Miss Johnston betrays no ready resentment. The Indian youths in their starched collars survey the scene as if it were still-life, which is exactly to what she has been able to reduce the spirit in this odd happening.

This is by no means to suggest that there lurks some secret, unsuspected or condign parody in Miss Johnston's prescient lens. She has merely the taste to arrange what she finds; her subjects, within her eyes, continue their essential lives, independent of her or our observation, locked in the suspension of time, like flies in amber, but nevertheless alive in the translucent air of history. They stand as metaphor or parable in their sturdy dreaminess, their selfless absorption in self-improvement. It is a measure of Miss Johnston's vision that she enables us to spy upon so many anonymous, long-vanished individuals, who still so vividly speak to us in public of their proper private longings for a shared social paradise. Despite her camera's candor, her entire incapacity to trim or trick, we must know it was not, nor by no means yet is, any earthly heaven. But she did capture, to an almost magical degree, the better part of an historic aspiration in its innocent and necessary striving.

The camera's authority, based on its assumption of immediate, boundless and ultimate verisimilitude, is a powerful instrument of indignation. Pictures of accidents and horrors, battlefields and lynchings have been so wastefully spent in their irresponsible and reckless pornography that we are now hard to interest, to say nothing of shock. Color has added no further dimension of convincing truth. Most reportage moves us chiefly to turn the page to one more picture. Images Miss Johnston found grip us by their soft, sweet monochrome. In them, hearts beat, breath is held; time ticks. Eyelids barely flutter. Outside of Hampton there is an ogre's world of cruel competition and insensate violence, but while we are here, all the fair words that have been spoken to the outcast and injured are true. Promises are kept. Hers is the promised land.

"The Old Folks at Home."

"A Hampton Graduate at home."

"The old-time cabin"

"A Hampton Graduate's home."

"The old well."

"The improved well. (three Hampton grandchildren.)"

"Saluting the Flag at the Whittier Primary School."

"Primary class studying plants. Whittier School."

"Kindergarten Children washing and ironing."

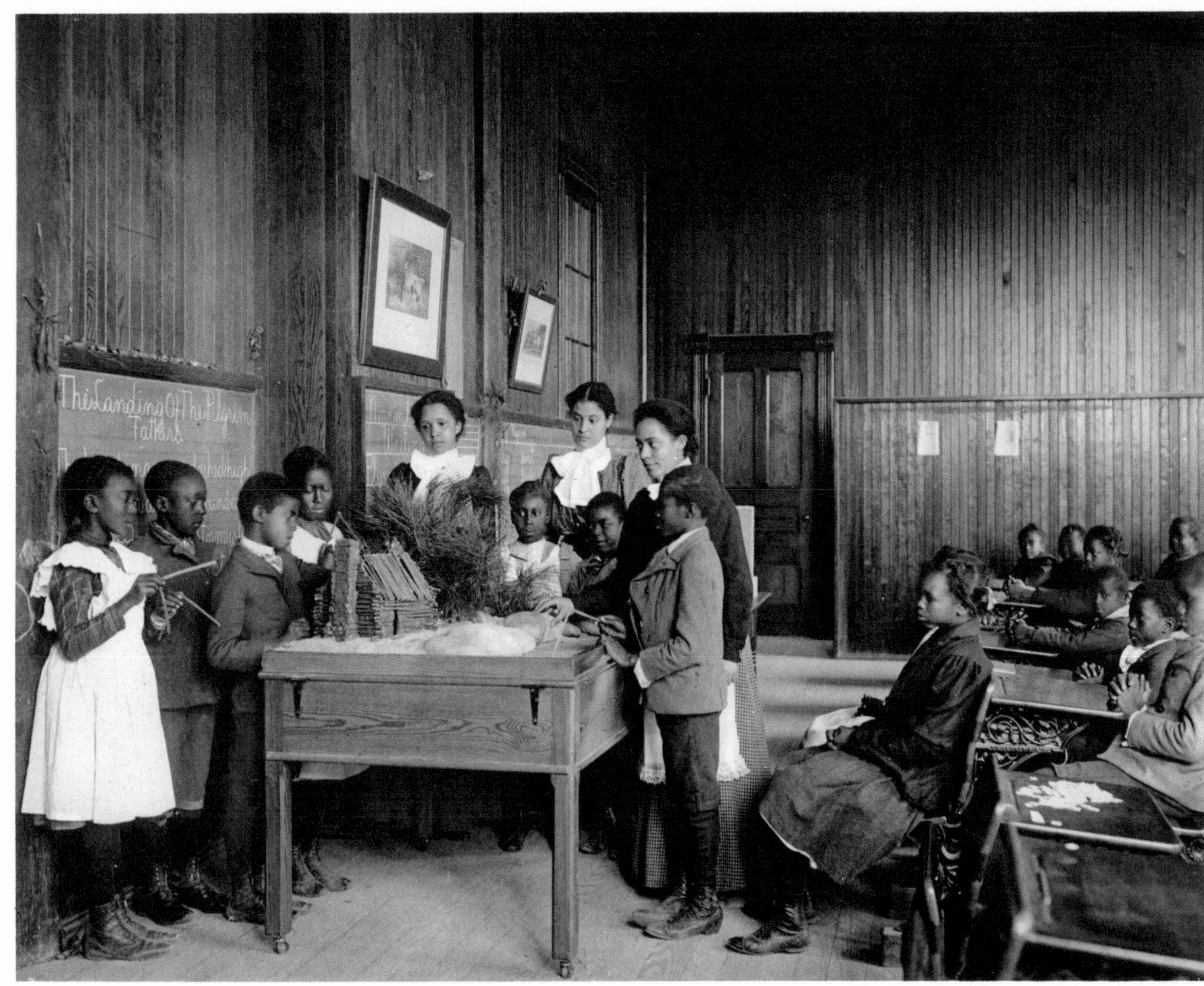

"Thanksgiving Day lesson at the Whittier."

FAR LEFT:
"Adele Quinney. Stockbridge tribe. A girl whose every physical measurement is artistically correct"

LEFT:
"John Wizi. Sioux. Son of Chief Wizi of Crow Creek. S. D."

"Class in American History."

"Geography.
Studying the Seasons."

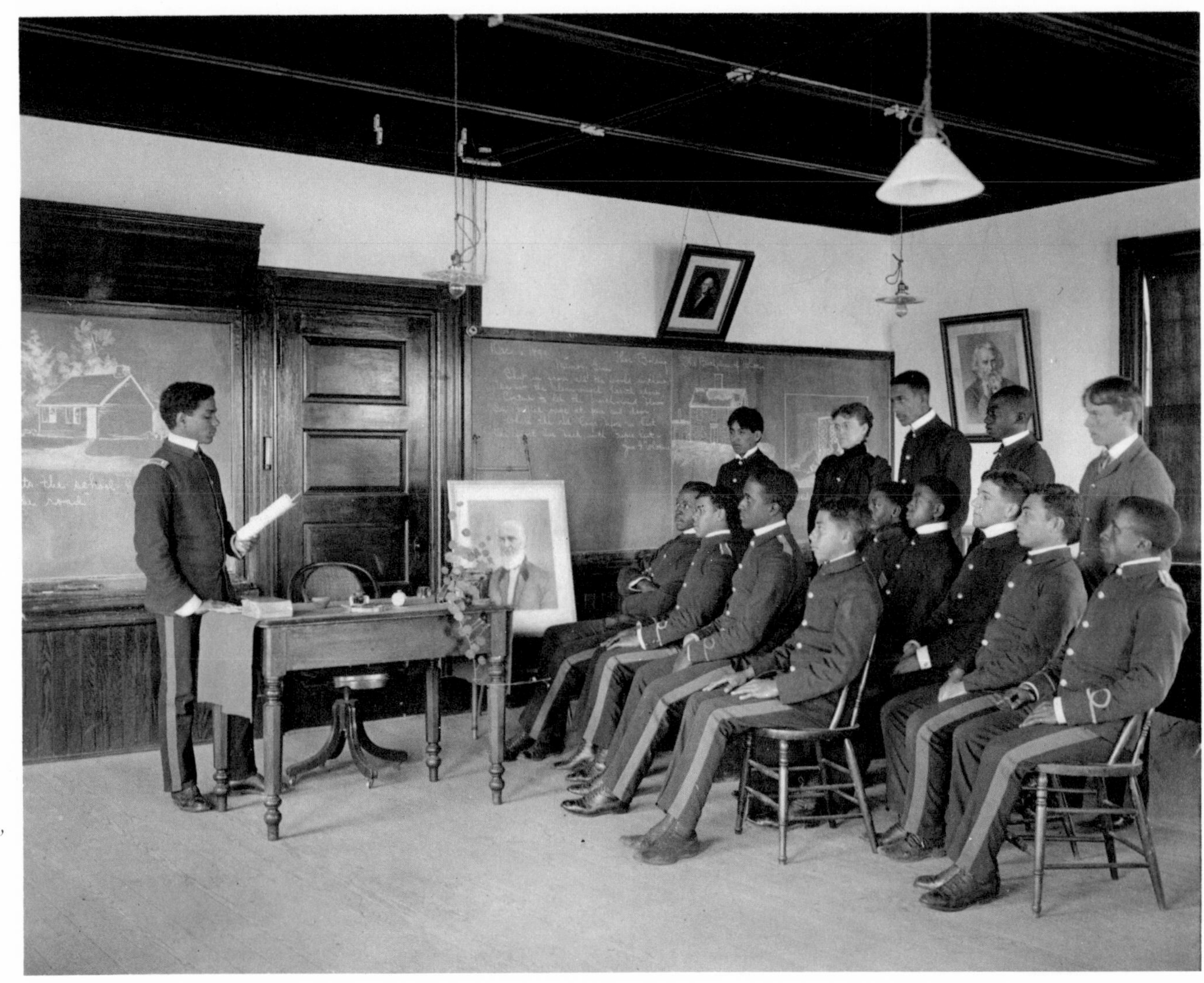

"Literature—Lesson on Whittier. Middle Class. 1899."

*"Geography.
Studying
the cathedral towns."*

"Field work in sketching. (Agriculture work.)"

"Geography. Lesson on land formation on the beach at Old Point."

"A sketch class at work."

"Arithmetic. Lesson under a student mason."

"Agriculture.
Plant life.
Study of plants
or a 'plant society'."

"Arithmetic. Measuring and pacing."

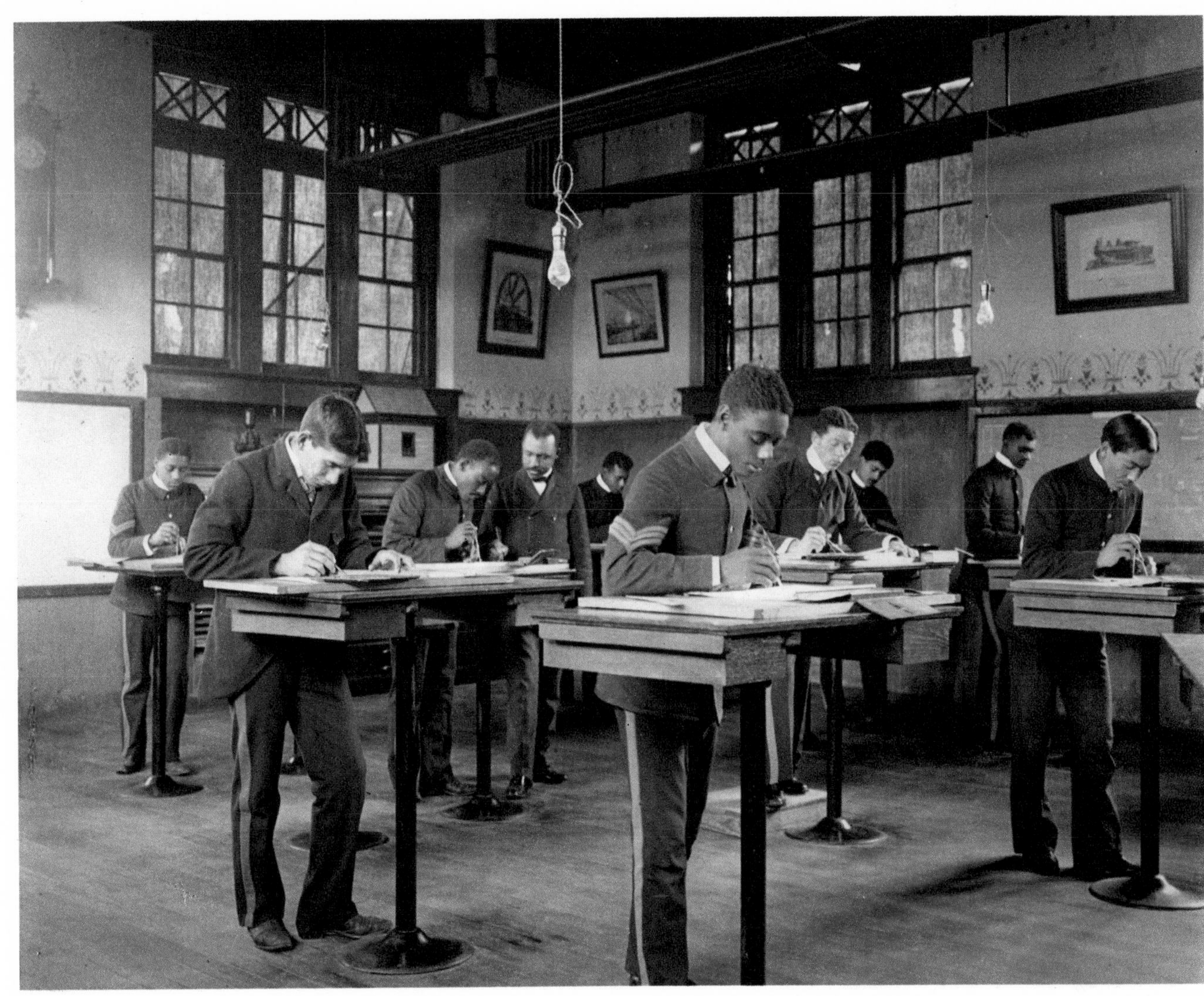

*"Trade School.
Mechanical drawing."*

"*Indian Orchestra.*"

"A Foot-ball Team."

*"Agriculture.
Plant life.
Studying the Seed."*

*"Agriculture.
Plant life.
Experiments with
plants and soil."*

*"History.
A class at Fort Monroe."*

*"Agriculture.
A class judging swine."*

"Physics.
The Screw
as applied to the
cheese press."

"Agriculture. Butter-making."

"*Agriculture.*
Animal life.
Studying the horse."

"Geography. Lesson on local industries—lumber and coal at School wharf."

*"Agriculture.
Sampling milk."*

"A class in manual training. Bent iron and tin."

"Trade School. Brick laying."

"Stairway of Treasurer's Residence. Students at work."

"A Class in dress-making."

*"Trade School.
Shoe-making."*

"Agriculture.
Mixing fertilizer."

"Serving the dinner."

"The Post-graduate Class of 1900."

A NOTE ON THE PHOTOGRAPHER

FRANCES BENJAMIN JOHNSTON was born in Grafton, West Virginia, January 15, 1864. *Who's Who* states she passed early years "on the banks of the Ohio River," in Rochester, New York, and Washington, D.C. She was educated first at Nôtre Dame Convent, Govanston, Maryland. At first she seems to have aimed at a writer's career, but in 1883 she went to Paris, where with many other young Americans she studied for two years at the Académie Julien, drawing and painting. She drew professionally enough to illustrate her early magazine stories, but journalistic illustration was rapidly changing from zinc line-cuts to half-tone photographic reproduction. She spent some time at the Art Students' League of Washington, D.C. (later incorporated in the Corcoran Gallery School) before deciding she wished to become a professional photographer. She first worked with commercial photographers, doing a considerable amount of architectural documentation, but became disgusted with the onerous hackwork of the plodding journeyman. So she apprenticed herself to Professor Thomas William Smillie, then in charge of the Division of Photography of The Smithsonian Institution. In 1890 she opened her own well-equipped studio in a picturesque low brick building at the end of a walled rose garden, once laid out by John Burroughs, the great naturalist, at the rear of 1332 V Street, N.W. She wrote to George Eastman in Rochester for advice as to the latest equipment and methods. Miss Johnston seems to have enjoyed immediate success, artistically and financially. This was due to her diligence and technical mastery, as well as to her social position, which embraced easy access to The White House from the administrations of Cleveland, Harrison, McKinley, through "Teddy" Roosevelt and Taft. She seems to have been particularly close to Mrs. Roosevelt and the whole Roosevelt family. Mrs. Cleveland and Mrs. McKinley came to her studio to pose, with their Cabinet ladies. Apart from her admirably schooled eye, she wrote that as far as technical aids went, she "depended entirely on Eikonogen"—a developing agent, now virtually obsolete. For the rest, ". . . one should go for inspiration to such masters as Rembrandt, Van Dyck, Sir Joshua Reynolds, Romney and Gainsborough, rather than to the compilers of chemical formulæ."

Pictures of her own studio, with its enormous northern skylight ("the finest portrait-light south of Philadelphia"), show a typical Bohemian residence of the Nineties, recalling the interiors of William Merritt Chase, complete with tiger rugs, paisley throws, Indian basketry, a plaster Venus de Milo, Parisian posters and oriental bric-a-brac.

In *Demorest's Family Magazine* of March 1892 she published an epoch-making picture story of a tour of the Pennsylvania coal fields. A photo-taking Ida Tarbell, she made a thorough investigation. "A subject I touch reluctantly is that of the innumerable risks and ever-present dangers. . . ." In spite of filthy mine shafts, deep and dangerous tunnels, she was relieved to note: "In their schools I found the miners' children neat, cleanly, and fresh-faced. . . ." Miss Johnston covered a number of stories involving fresh-faced youngsters before coming to Hampton, when she recorded the educational systems of Washington, D.C., West Point, Annapolis, and later Carlisle, the Indian college, and Tuskegee. She also photographed the unique collection of Barye animal bronzes in the Corcoran Gallery, a Lynn, Massachusetts shoe factory, the Mammoth Cave, "Some White House Orchids," the United States Mint, "A Day At Niagara," and, for *The Ladies' Home Journal,* "What A Woman Can Do With A Camera." Also for the *Journal* (February 1900) she illustrated the story by Jacob A. Riis, himself a notable documentary photographer, on "President Roosevelt's children," which brought her much attention.

She was commissioned by a news syndicate and took over 150 pictures of Admiral George Dewey on the flagship U.S.S. "Olympia," on his triumphal return voyage around the world after the battle of Manila. She caught up with the Great White Fleet as it lay anchored in the Bay of Naples in 1899. (A letter from the Governor of New York and former Assistant Secretary of the Navy, Theodore Roosevelt, provided the magical introduction.) From such assignments she became known as the unofficial "Photographer to the American Court." Later, she preserved for posterity interiors and exteriors of the millionaires' palaces built by Carrère and Hastings and McKim, Mead & White. Through her lens, we know what the early interiors decorated by Elsie de Wolfe looked like, as well as the Astor and Vanderbilt mansions. Sometimes she enraged her patrons by chasing them out of their own homes when she was at work; once she ordered a tree cut down when it blocked her view of a Colonial church in Williamsburg. In 1892 she was in Chicago, chronicling "The Evolution Of A Great Exhibition" (as Assistant Photographer to the United States Government) and, in this capacity, she took the group portrait of the delegates signing the Spanish-American peace protocol, which formed the basis of Theodore Chartran's famous commissioned painting of this event. In her V Street studio she stored some 5,000 plates. At present, apart from the huge collection of negatives now in the Library of Congress, there are some 1,200 of her portraits taken between 1880 and 1910 in the Huntington Library, San Marino, California.

For the Paris Universal Exposition of 1900, marking the birth of a new century and era, she was commissioned by the Reverend Hollis Burke Frissell, General Armstrong's able successor at Hampton, to take more than 150 pictures of the Institute. She had already just made 350 camera studies of the public school system of the nation's capital, at the rate of fifteen prints a day. She exposed two shots of every pose, just in case. Her ability to seize group portraits and to hold the rigid attention of children of difficult ages was early appreciated. She disclaimed all gadgetry and special equipment in company with the best of subsequent news photographers.

It was stated in *The Southern Workman and Hampton School Record* (January 1900) that: "The value of such an exhibit lies not only in showing to others but in making clear to the school itself what it is doing. . . . This collection of pictures, arranged by subjects and mounted on the movable leaves of a large upright cabinet, will form part of the Negro exhibit in Paris, to be under the care of Mr. T. J. Calloway, a young colored man who has been associated with Mr. Washington at Tuskegee. . . ." The exhibit consisted of original photographs only; there was no space in the American Pavilion for actual examples of the manual and domestic arts which Hampton professed. The Pavilion was situated "on the Seine River, on the *Street of Nations*; it is conceived in the style of a majestic Pantheon. . . . The principal body of the structure is surmounted by a cupola of 20 metres topped by an American eagle which seems about to launch itself to conquer the world. . . ." Miss Johnston was the only American woman invited to attend the Third International Photographic Congress, held as an adjunct to the Exposition. In her excellent French she spoke on the work of American artist-photographers. Her work won her the Grand Prix, medals, world acclaim and the fair repute of Hampton. Calloway reported: "It was the general opinion that nowhere had the photographer's lens been so eloquent and impressive in the story of a great work as was silently narrated by these photographs."

Her life into the twentieth century was, if anything, even busier. It is not the place here to chronicle her devoted coverage of Colonial and Federal architecture, which has already been gratefully noted by Mr. Paul Vanderbilt (*The Journal of The American Institute of Architects,* November 1952). He knew her well towards the end of her life when he was Consultant in Iconography at the Library of Congress. It was an accepted convention at the time "that if anything notable were to happen, she would be present." She became a determined, irascible little old lady. During the First World War she had photographed a bridge and spent a night in jail for "spying." Her prices were high (for a woman); she was actively in competition with her male colleagues. Poor at business, she rarely opened, and seldom paid, her bills. She kept everything she ever owned, moving the mass along with her as she moved. She fueded with martial regularity with the Department of Internal Revenue. She loved flattery, was enormously proud of her accomplishment both as woman and artist. A considerable body of documentary evidence, apart from her own plates, awaits definitive biography. Mr. Vanderbilt also tells us: "She was interested, too, in recording structures in disrepair or obscured by alteration before they should disappear altogether, and was remarkably successful in arousing local interest in rediscovering and paying attention to such situations. . . ."

In 1945 she was made an Honorary Member of the American Institute of Architects. Aged 88, she died in New Orleans in 1952.

THIS BOOK HAS BEEN PRINTED FOR THE MUSEUM OF MODERN ART BY PHOTOGRAVURE AND COLOR, MOONACHIE, NEW JERSEY. THE PAPER IS MOHAWK SUPERFINE TEXT, EGGSHELL. TYPEFACES USED ARE CRAW MODERN AND MONOPHOTO BEMBO. TYPOGRAPHY IS BY JOSEPH BOURKE DEL VALLE.